Good Character Traits

Honesty

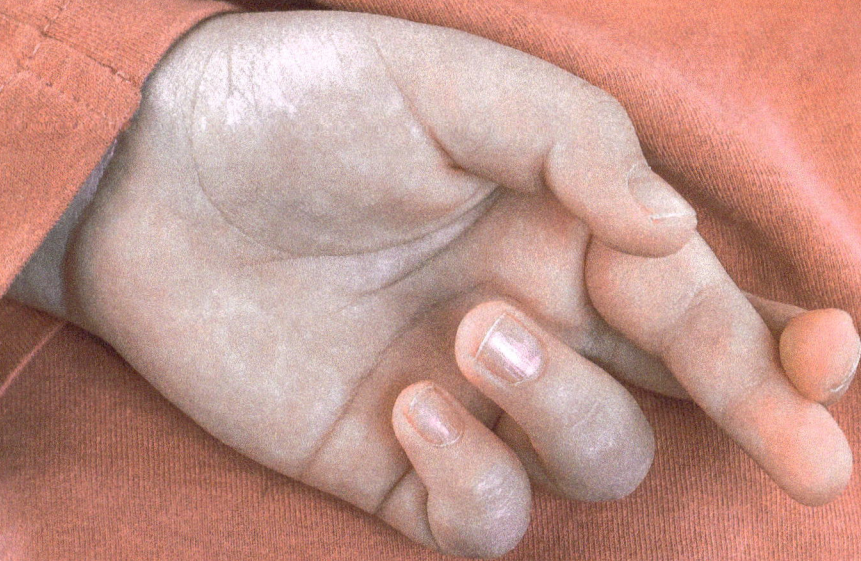

Ashley Lee

e→ Explore other books at:
WWW.ENGAGEBOOKS.COM

VANCOUVER, B.C.

WWW.ENGAGEBOOKS.COM

Honesty: Good Character Traits
Lee, Ashley, 1995 –
Text © 2024 Engage Books
Design © 2024 Engage Books

Edited by: A.R. Roumanis
Design by: Mandy Christiansen

Text set in Myriad Pro Regular.
Chapter headings set in Anton.

FIRST EDITION / FIRST PRINTING

LIBRARY AND ARCHIVES CANADA CATALOGUING IN PUBLICATION

Title: Honesty / Ashley Lee.
Names: Lee, Ashley, author.
Description: Series statement: Good Character Traits

Identifiers: Canadiana (print) 20230446973 | Canadiana (ebook) 20230446981
ISBN 978-1-77878-659-4 (hardcover)
ISBN 978-1-77878-660-0 (softcover)
ISBN 978-1-77878-661-7 (epub)
ISBN 978-1-77878-662-4 (pdf)

This project has been made possible in part by the Government of Canada.

Canada

Honesty

Contents

What Is Honesty?

Honesty means telling the truth.

It means not hiding **important** things.

Key Word

Important: something that is special or needed.

Why Is Honesty Important?

Being honest helps people **trust** you.

Key Word

Trust: the feeling that someone is there for you and believes in you.

Trust is what makes someone a good friend.

What Does Honesty Look Like?

Honest people tell the truth even when it is hard.

They do not **pretend** or make up stories.

Key Word

Pretend: act as if something is true when it is not.

How Does Honesty Affect You?

Not telling the truth can make you feel **guilty**.

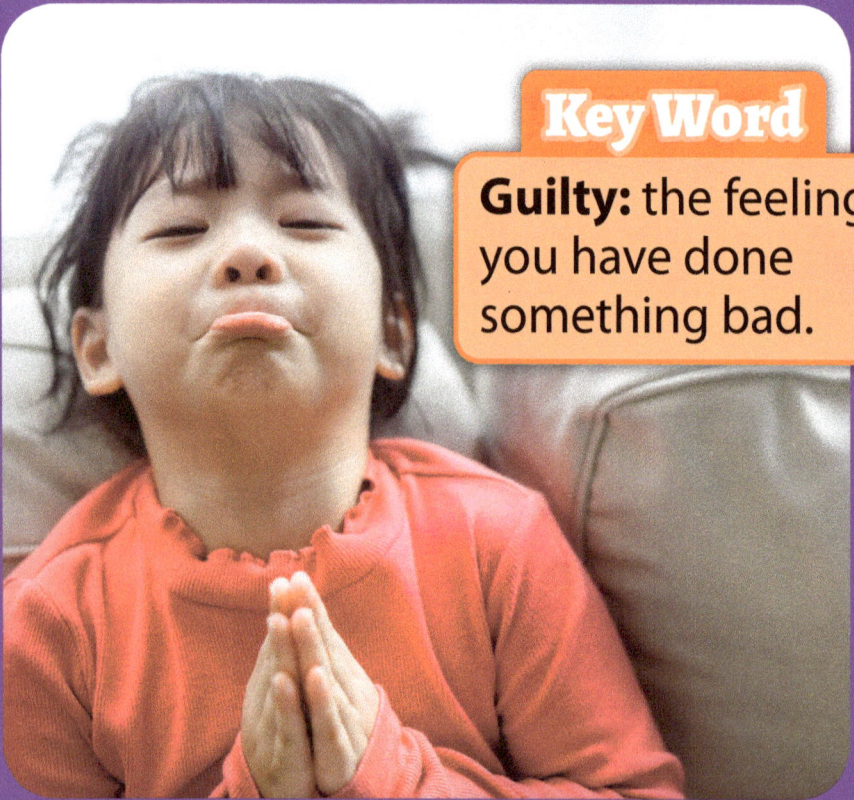

Guilty: the feeling you have done something bad.

Telling the truth can make you feel better.

How Does Honesty Affect Others?

Not telling the truth can hurt people.

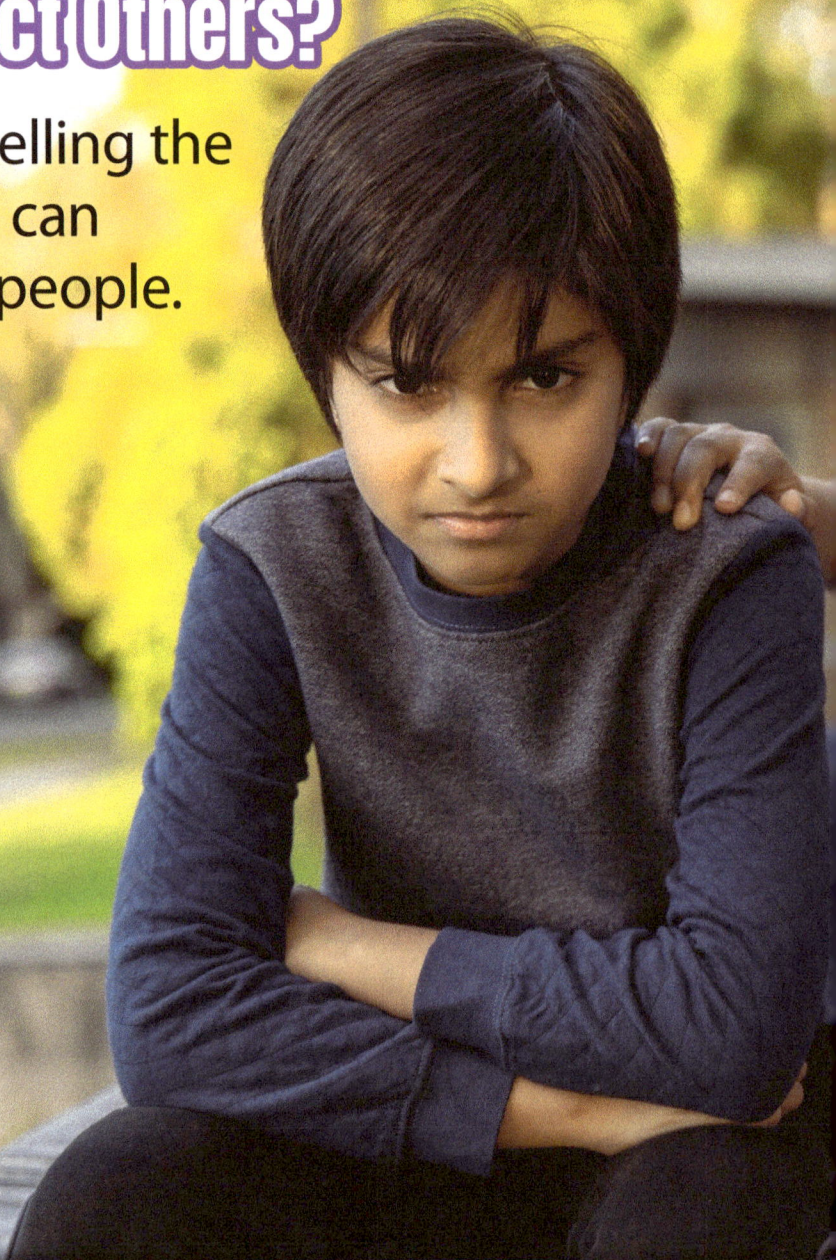

Being honest stops people from being hurt.

Is Everyone Honest?

Some people tell lots of **lies**.

I didn't do that!

I can jump 10 feet in the air!

Key Word

Lies: things that are not true.

Sometimes telling a lie is just a **mistake**.

I have a pet lion!

I have read every book in the library.

Key Word

Mistake: something that someone did wrong.

15

Is It Bad if You Are Not Honest?

Telling a lie does not make you a bad person.

But you should always
try to be honest so you
do not hurt other people.

Does Honesty Change Over Time?

Most people become more honest as they get older.

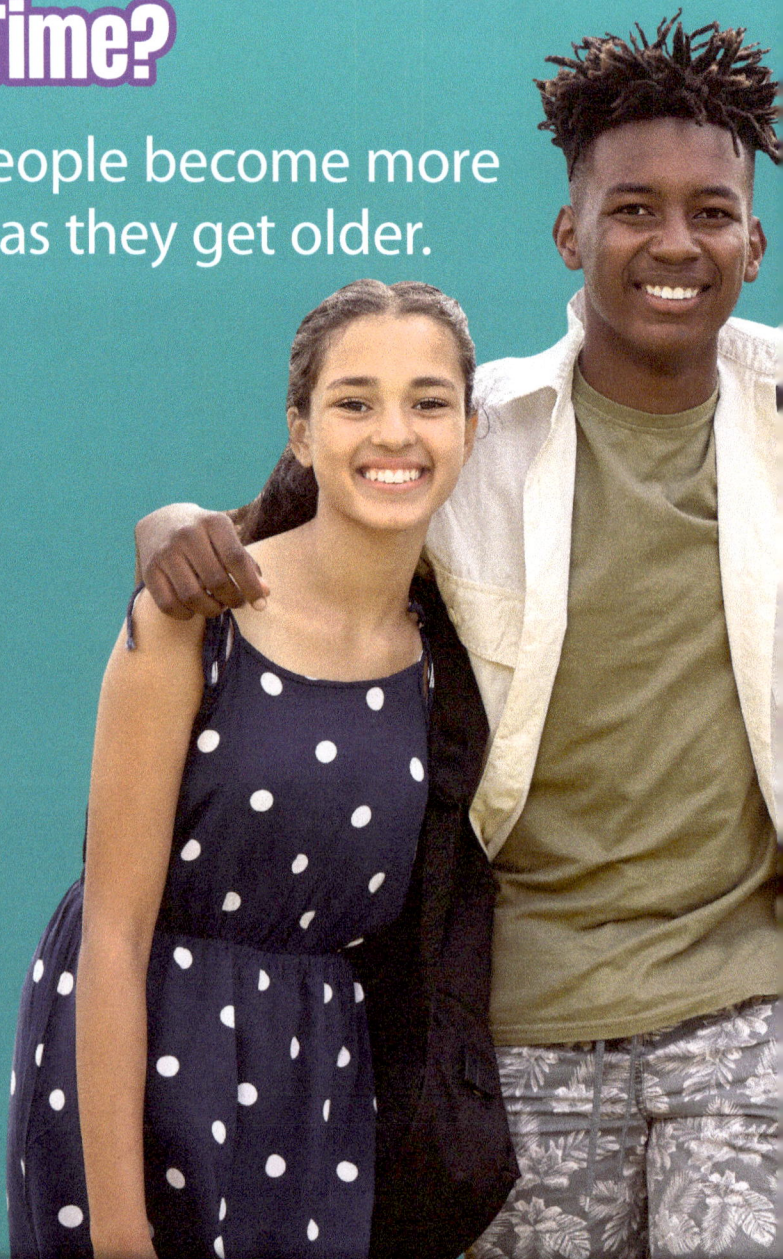

They learn how telling lies can hurt others.

Is It Hard to Be Honest?

It can be hard to be honest if you are afraid of getting in trouble.

It is easier to be honest when you learn that it is okay to make mistakes.

How Can You Learn to Be More Honest?

Think before you speak. Ask yourself if what you are saying is true.

Be honest even when it is hard.

How Can You Help Others Be More Honest?

Be an **example** to other people by always telling the truth.

Key Word

Example: a way to show something to help someone understand.

Thank other people for being honest with you.

How to Be Honest Every Day

1. **Admit** when you are wrong.

2. Speak the truth in a kind way.

Key Word

Admit: say the truth about something.

3. Do what you said you were going to do.

4. Know that it is okay to make mistakes.

Honesty Around the World

People lose things every day all over the world.

Other people find these things. They give them to the police instead of taking them.

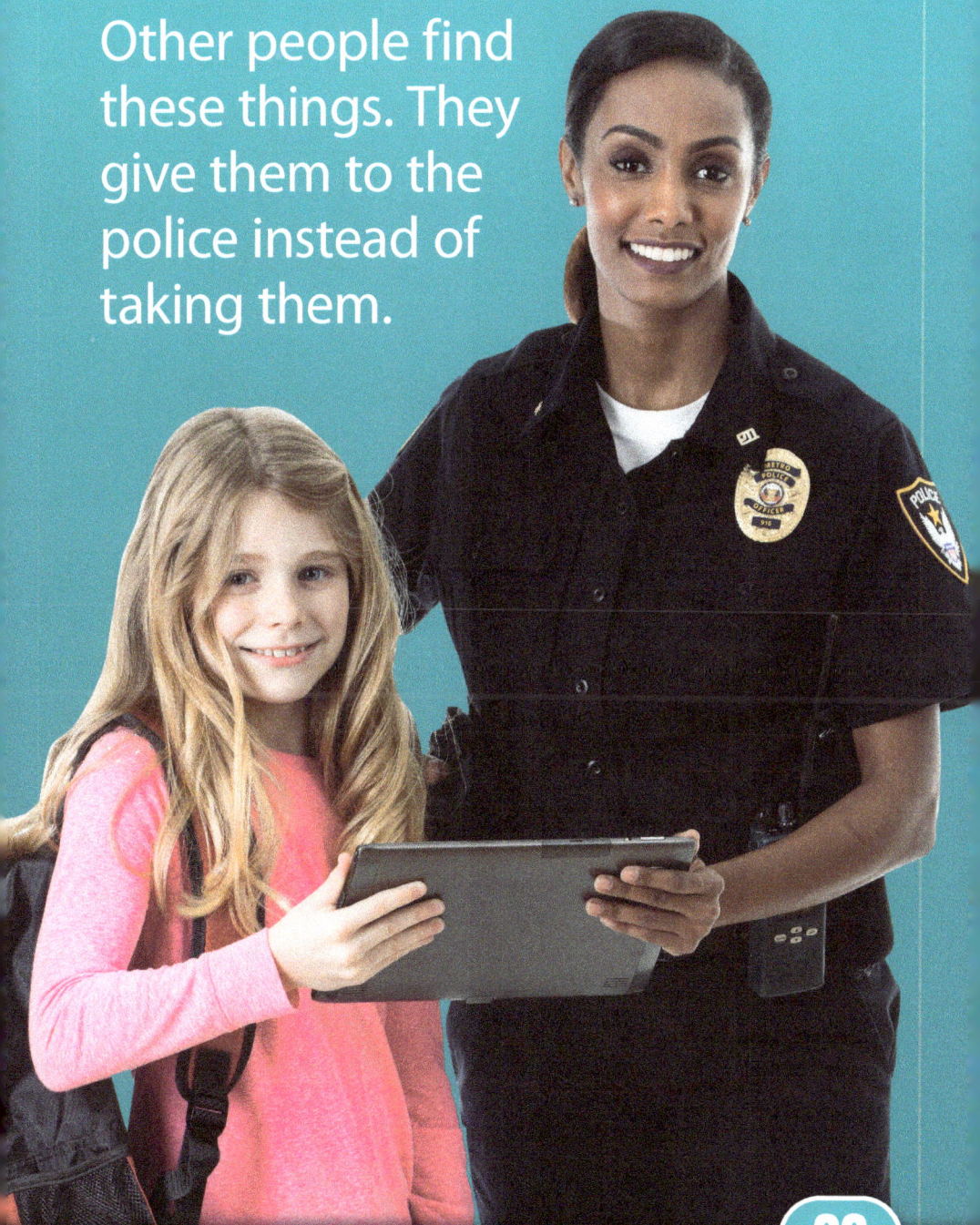

Quiz

Test your knowledge of honesty by answering the following questions. The questions are based on what you have read in this book. The answers are listed on the bottom of the next page.

1 Does being honest help people trust you?

2 Do honest people pretend or make up stories?

3 Can telling the truth make you feel better?

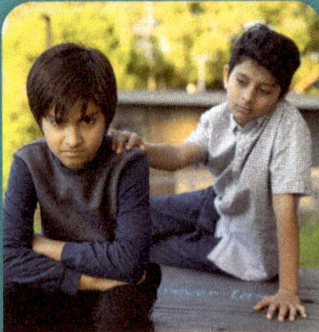

4 Can lying hurt people?

5 Does lying make you a bad person?

6 Should you admit when you are wrong?

Explore Other Level 1 Readers.

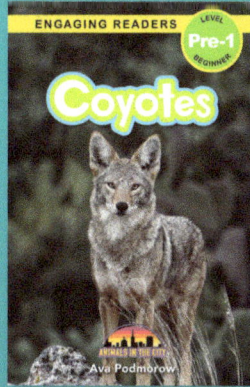

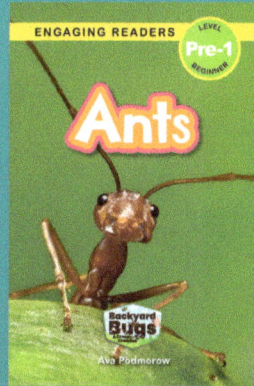

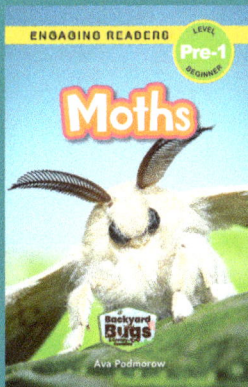

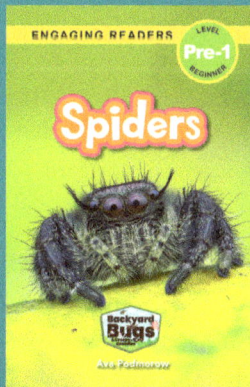

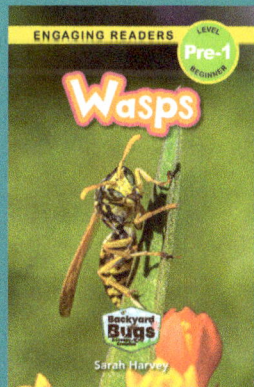

ENGAGING READERS — LEVEL Pre-1 BEGINNER — **Cats** — Ava Podmorow — ANIMALS IN THE CITY

ENGAGING READERS — LEVEL Pre-1 BEGINNER — **Coyotes** — Ava Podmorow — ANIMALS IN THE CITY

ENGAGING READERS — LEVEL Pre-1 BEGINNER — **Owls** — Ava Podmorow — ANIMALS IN THE CITY

ENGAGING READERS — LEVEL Pre-1 BEGINNER — **Raccoons** — Sarah Harvey — ANIMALS IN THE CITY

ENGAGING READERS — LEVEL Pre-1 BEGINNER — **Skunks** — Ava Podmorow — ANIMALS IN THE CITY

ENGAGING READERS — LEVEL Pre-1 BEGINNER — **Ants** — Ava Podmorow — Backyard Bugs

ENGAGING READERS — LEVEL Pre-1 BEGINNER — **Moths** — Ava Podmorow — Backyard Bugs

ENGAGING READERS — LEVEL Pre-1 BEGINNER — **Spiders** — Ava Podmorow — Backyard Bugs

ENGAGING READERS — LEVEL Pre-1 BEGINNER — **Wasps** — Sarah Harvey — Backyard Bugs

Visit www.engagebooks.com/readers

www.ingramcontent.com/pod-product-compliance
Lightning Source LLC
Chambersburg PA
CBHW051237020426
42331CB00016B/3410